School Dinners Recipes

Old school recipes of the 1960s, 1970s and 1980s

By

Sally Berry

Published by Spellmagick Publishing

Contents

Introduction

One of the abiding memories of anyone who went to a British school in the 60's, 70's or 80's has to be school dinners. Many of us have fond memories of delights such as chocolate concrete, cornflake pie, butterscotch tart and pink custard, and not so fond memories of soggy semolina, lumpy mash and the unmistakable aroma of cheese and potato pie.

School dinners were a British institution, simple and filling recipes designed to fuel generations of learners. Real food, cooked from scratch using basic ingredients. We didn't always appreciate them at the time, they were often something to be endured before we were free to go out onto the playing fields with our friends.

Yet looking back, who can fail to feel a twinge of nostalgia at the thought of mashed potato being served with an ice cream scoop or huge jugs of mint custard complete with skin waiting to be poured over a stodgy belly filling pudding.

The recipes that follow are authentic school dinner recipes scaled down for the home cook. We hope you enjoy this trip down memory lane.

CHEESE AND POTATO PIE

Love it or hate it, this pie was one of the staples of school dinners in the 1970's. We always knew when it was cheese and potato pie day by the smell which seemed to pervade the whole school!

Ingredients: (Serves Four)

500g potatoes, peeled and cut into large chunks
150g grated cheese
25g butter
1 onion finely chopped
2 tbsp oil
1 egg
Sliced tomato to garnish (optional but authentic!)

Method:

Preheat the oven to gas mark 6 / 200c.

Place the potatoes into a pan of salted water, bring to the boil and cook until soft

Meanwhile, fry the onion in the butter.

Drain the potatoes but leave them in the pan. Add the fried onion, cheese, oil and egg. Mash together thoroughly or for added authenticity leave in a few lumps!

Place the mixture in an ovenproof dish or divide into four individual dishes. Slice the tomato if using and arrange over the top.

Bake for 20-30 minutes until golden.

TOAD IN THE HOLE

Classic British comfort food at its best, this simple recipe is a doddle to make. No toads were injured in the making of this dish.

Ingredients: (Serves Four)

8 pork sausages
1 tbsp vegetable oil
225g plain flour
4 eggs
250ml milk
salt and pepper to taste

Method:

Preheat the oven to 200 degrees C /gas mark 6.

Fry the sausages lightly in a pan with the oil until they are barely cooked. Alternatively, arrange the sausages in a baking dish in a single layer and pour the oil over them. Cook for 10 mins in the preheated oven.

Sieve the flour into a bowl and add the eggs and half the milk. Whisk together until smooth. Slowly add the remainder of the milk to form a smooth batter. Season with salt and pepper to taste.

Arrange the sausages in the baking dish and pour over the batter. Bake for 35 -40 minutes or until the centre is risen and brown.

SPAM FRITTERS

Ingredients: (Serves Four)

1 340g tin of Spam
125g plain flour
pinch of salt
4 fluid ounces of milk

oil for either shallow frying or deep frying

Method:

Sieve the flour into a bowl. Add a pinch of salt to taste. Whisk in the milk. The mixture should be quite thick.

Slice the spam into 8 pieces.

Heat the oil either in a frying pan or deep fat fryer depending on the cooking method being used. Oil temperature should be about 170C/350F. Test the temperature with cubes of bread.

Drop the spam slices into the batter and coat them well. Drop them into the hot oil for three to four minutes turning over as needed. This batter tends to soak up a lot of oil so drain well on paper towels.

IRISH STEW

Ingredients:

2 ½ lbs boned lamb or mutton
4 large potatoes
2 onions
4 carrots
2 cups water
salt and pepper to season

Method:

Cut the meat into chunks

Peel all the vegetables and slice into chunky pieces.

Layer the ingredients into a large saucepan starting with the potatoes.

Pour over the water and season to taste.

Leave to simmer on a very low light for 1 ½ to 2 ½ hours until the meat is tender and well cooked. You can also slow cook this dish in a casserole dish in a low oven or in a slow cooker.

Serve with dumplings (see the recipe on the next page)

DUMPLINGS

Fluffy balls of loveliness to accompany a hearty stew.

Ingredients: (Makes 8)

100g self-raising flour
50g suet
½ tsp salt
Cold water to mix

Method:

Mix the flour, suet and salt with water to make a firm but soft dough. Divide into 8 pieces. Drop into the stew around 20 minutes before the end of cooking time
For extra light dumplings, always add them to a boiling stew and never open the lid during the cooking time.

GOULASH

This Hungarian favourite managed to earn a place on the menu at many British schools in the late 1970's and early 1980's.

Ingredients: (Serves 4)

500g stewing steak
salt and pepper to taste
oil for frying
1 medium onion, chopped
3 cloves garlic, chopped
1 tin of plum tomatoes
3 beef stock cubes
1.2L (2 pints) boiling water
1 bay leaf
1 – 2 tsp paprika – or more if you like it spicy
1 tsp cayenne pepper, or to taste
3 potatoes, peeled and cut into chunks
2 carrots, sliced
flour for dusting

Method:

Dust the stewing steak with a little flour. Place a little oil in a large saucepan, season with salt and pepper and fry the steak until nearly brown.

Add the garlic and onion and sizzle until soft.

Make up the stock cubes with 2 pints of boiling water. Add this, together with the tomatoes, bay

leaf, paprika and cayenne to the saucepan.
Season again if desired.

Bring to the boil and simmer for 2 hours.

Add the potatoes and carrots and simmer for
another hour or until the veg is cooked.

SHEPHERDS PIE

Ingredients:

500g minced lamb
1 onion chopped
4 carrots chopped
2 garlic (cloves), crushed
500ml stock
½ a 400g tin of chopped tomatoes or a good dollop of tomato puree
1 tbsp Worcestershire sauce
1 tsp mixed herbs
850g potatoes
25g butter
100g cheddar cheese, grated optional

Method:

Preheat oven to 180'C/Gas mark 4/350F.

Brown the meat in a large frying pan. Add onions, garlic and carrots and cook through until the onion goes pale and transparent.

Stir in the stock and tomatoes/puree and bring to the boil. Add the Worcestershire sauce and mixed herbs and then simmer gently for 30 minutes.

Meanwhile boil the potatoes, cook until tender, drain and mash with the butter.

Place the meat into an ovenproof dish.   Spread over the mashed potato and top with cheese if using.

Cook in the oven for 30 minutes until the top is brown and crispy.

Note: For a Cottage Pie, substitute the lamb for beef.

OLD SCHOOL CURRY

This retro recipe works particularly well with left over chicken, turkey or beef but you can use fresh meat cut into cubes if you wish. If using fresh meat, fry in a pan until nearly cooked through and then add it to the mixture when it begins to simmer.

Ingredients: (Serves 2)

2 onions finely chopped
1 clove garlic
2 tbsp curry powder
1 tbsp flour
2 cloves
1 tbsp tomato puree
1/4 tsp ground ginger
1/4 tsp cinnamon
2 tbsp mango chutney
1 tbsp lemon juice
3 tbsp sugar
1/2-pint water
1/2 tsp salt

Method:

In a large pan fry onion and garlic together until soft and translucent.

Add curry powder and flour, cloves, tomato puree, ginger, cinnamon, mango chutney, lemon juice and sugar.

Cook through for a minute and add the water. Bring to the boil then turn down the heat until the mixture simmers. If using fresh meat which you have pre-fried add this now.

Simmer for one hour. If you are using left-over cooked meat, add this ten minutes before the end of cooking time. Ensure the meat is cooked through and piping hot.

FARMHOUSE MINCE

Ingredients: (Serves 4)

500g minced beef
1 onion
150ml water
1 tin condensed vegetable soup
5 carrots
3 parsnips
3 potatoes

Method:

Finely chop the onion. Peel and chop the carrots, parsnips and potatoes into chunks of about 2.5 cm.

Add all of the ingredients into a casserole dish or ovenproof dish. This dish can also be cooked in a slow cooker.

Set the oven to 170C/Gas Mark 4/350F. Cook for 1 – 1 ½ hour or until the veg is soft.

MACARONI CHEESE

Ingredients: (Serves 2)

250g macaroni
1 tbsp butter
1 tbsp plain flour
450ml milk
black pepper
1 tsp mustard powder
200g grated cheddar cheese

Method:

Cook the macaroni as directed on the packet and drain well.

Melt the butter in a saucepan, add the flour and stir well to form a roux. Season to taste with black pepper, add the mustard powder and stir over a low heat for one minute.

Add the milk a little at a time, work in well with a whisk. If you add the milk too quickly the mixture will curdle so work slowly and keep whisking.

Once the milk is all incorporated bring the mixture to the boil stirring all the time. Add the cheese, stir for another minute and then add the macaroni.

Serve as is, or place in dish, sprinkle with more cheese and brown in the oven – 180C/Gas Mark 5/375F

FISHERMANS PIE

Ingredients: (Serves 4)

1kg potatoes
knob of butter
400g white fish filleted and diced
25g butter
25g plain flour
4 spring onions finely chopped
400ml milk
1 tsp mustard
ground black pepper
grated cheddar

Method:

Preheat the oven to 200C/Gas Mark 6/400F. Peel and slice the potatoes and place them in a saucepan. Cover them with water and bring to the boil.

When the potatoes are cooked and tender, drain them and mash them well with a knob of butter and season with black pepper.

Meanwhile, melt the butter in a saucepan and gradually add in the flour then add the spring onions. Cook for one minute.

Slowly add in the milk, whisking well to avoid lumps. Cook for around five minutes or until the mixture has thickened.

Add the fish and the mustard and stir well. Spoon this mixture into an ovenproof dish.

Top with the mashed potato and top with a little grated cheese.

Bake for 25 minutes or until the top is golden.

CORNISH PASTIES

Ingredients: (Makes 4)

For the Pastry
250 g plain flour
60 g margarine
65 g lard
2 tbsp water
beaten egg or a little milk to glaze

For the Filling:
250 g minced beef
1 medium onion finely chopped
100 g diced raw potato
1 carrot diced
½ tsp salt
½ tsp black pepper

Method:

Preheat the oven to 220 °C/ Gas 7/425F

Sieve the flour into a bowl, rub in the fat until the mixture resembles breadcrumbs. Slowly add enough cold water for the mixture to form a soft dough.

Roll the pastry out onto a floured surface and divide into four pieces. Roll each piece out into a circle about the size of a saucer.

Fry the beef with the onion until the onion becomes soft, season with salt and black pepper and add the potato and carrot.

Put a quarter of this mixture into one half of each pastry circle. Damp the edges with water and fold the other half of the pastry over the filling. Pinch the edges to seal.

Brush with beaten egg or milk to glaze and bake for 30-40 minutes until golden brown.

CHEESE FOOTBALLS

Ingredients:

140g plain flour
70g of margarine
3 eggs beaten
330ml water
110g grated cheese
½ tsp mustard powder
pinch of salt
Oil for deep frying

Method·

Place the margarine, water and salt into a saucepan and bring to the boil. Remove from the heat and add all of the flour.

Beat well until the mixture forms a ball and leaves the side of the pan. Allow to cool a little, then turn into a bowl and add the eggs, then beat well until the mixture is soft and smooth.

Stir in the cheese and mustard powder, flour your hands and form into small balls.

Heat the oil in a deep fat fryer or chip pan to 360F then drop the balls into the fat to fry. Remove when golden brown and drain on kitchen paper.

STOVIES

Ingredients:

4-5 large potatoes
2 onions
8 sausages or 225g sausage meat or any cooked meat
salt and pepper

Method:

Peel and slice the potatoes into ½ cm slices. Roughly chop the onions. Mix the potatoes and onions together and season with salt and pepper.

Barely cover the base of a heavy bottomed saucepan with water (approx. 1/2cm) and cover with the potato mixture.

Cut up the sausages or meat and place on top of the potato.

Put the lid on the pan and heat up gently. Once the mixture is heated through turn the heat to a low light and then cook for 30 minutes.

Try not to take the lid off too often during cooking but check the potatoes are not burning or drying out occasionally. Shake the pan to stop the stovies sticking.

MEAT LOAF

Ingredients:

454g minced beef
225g sausage meat
250g dried breadcrumbs
1 egg beaten
330ml milk
½ onion
¼ tsp mustard power
¼ tsp black pepper
½ tsp sage

Method:

Preheat the oven to 180C/Gas Mark 4/350F.

Combine all the ingredients in a large bowl.

Transfer to a 2lb loaf tin. Bake in the oven for 1 to
1 ½ hours until cooked through.

COWBOY HOTPOT

Ingredients: (serves 4)

700g mince
2 onions roughly chopped
400g carrots roughly chopped
1 tin sweetcorn
700g potatoes chopped into chunks
1.2l beef stock
4 tbsp tomato puree
2 x 415g tins baked beans
dash of tabacoo Sauce
salt and pepper to season
oil to fry mince

Method:

Place the oil in a large saucepan and gently fry the mince with the onions for 4 -5 minutes. Add the carrots and potatoes.

Add the tomato puree and stock, bring to the boil and simmer until the veg is tender.

Add the baked beans, sweetcorn and tabasco sauce and season with salt and pepper.

Cook through for 5-10 minutes and serve.

CORNED BEEF HASH

Ingredients:

400g potatoes
1 tin corned beef
1 tin baked beans
1 onion chopped
2 tbsp tomato ketchup
knob of butter
salt and black pepper
splash of worcestershire sauce
grated cheese (optional)

Method:
Put the potatoes on to boil until soft. Drain well and mash with the butter until no lumps remain. Season with salt and black pepper.

Lightly fry the onion in a little butter. Open the corned beef and crumble into the pan with the onion. Fry for a minute or two.

Preheat the oven to 180C/Gas Mark 4/350C. Prepare an ovenproof dish. Mix the ketchup and baked beans together, add a splash of Worcestershire sauce and mix into the corned beef and onion mixture. Spread over the base of the ovenproof dish.

Spread the mashed potato on top of the corned beef mixture, sprinkle with grated cheese (optional) and bake for 30 minutes until top is brown and crisp.

SAUSAGE MEAT PIE

Ingredients:
450g sausage meat
1 egg beaten
175g lard
85g packet sage and onion stuffing mix
350g plain flour
1 tbsp French mustard

Method:

Place the flour into a bowl and rub in the lard until the mixture resembles breadcrumbs. Stir in enough cold water to form a fairly stiff dough, knead lightly and then rest in the fridge for 30 minutes.

Preheat the oven to 190C/Gas Mark 5/400F. Make up the stuffing according to the instructions on the packet and set aside to cool.

Using two thirds of the pastry, line a 19cm round sandwich tin. Combine the sausage meat, stuffing and mustard together and spread over the pastry base.

Roll out the remaining pastry to form a lid for the pie. Wet the edges and seal well. Brush the top with beaten egg.

Bake for 45 minutes until golden brown.

MINT CUSTARD

Ingredients:

300 ml whole milk
2 tbsp caster sugar
20 g cornflour
A few drops of peppermint extract
A few drops of green food colouring

Method:

Measure the milk into a jug

In a separate bowl mix together the cornflour and sugar. Add a small amount of milk a tablespoon full at a time until the mixture forms a smooth paste. Place the remaining milk into a pan then add the paste mixture. Bring slowly to the boil stirring well all the time.

Once the mixture starts to thicken, add the peppermint essence to taste and a few drops of food colouring.

CHOCOLATE CONCRETE

Ingredients:

200g plain flour
200g sugar
100g butter
50g cocoa powder

Method:

Preheat the oven to 180 C/Gas Mark 4/350 F

Mix the dry ingredients in a bowl. Melt the butter and mix into the dry ingredients.

Work the mixture with your fingers until it resembles a crumble type consistency.

Press into a greased tin. Bake for approx. 20 mins. Sprinkle with sugar and serve with mint custard!

MANCHESTER TART

Ingredients:

25g sugar
1 desiccated coconut
100g butter or margarine
1 jar jam
225g plain flour
1 banana
30ml water
230ml custard

Method:

Preheat oven to 190C/Gas Mark 5/375 F
First, make the pastry. Place the flour into a bowl
and rub in the margarine. Once the mixture
resembles fine breadcrumbs, stir in the sugar.

Add enough cold water to make the mixture come
together to form a soft dough using a knife to mix.
Turn out onto a floured surface.

Roll out the dough to line a sandwich tin.

Bake blind for 20 minutes. If you don't have the
ceramic baking beans to bake the pastry blind, then
cut out a circle of greaseproof paper the same size
as your baking tin and place a layer of dried beans
or rice on top.

Five minutes before the end of cooking time
remove the paper and rice or beans to allow the
pastry to become golden brown.

Once the pastry has cooled, make the filling.

You can use a premade custard out of a tin or jar but some people find this too thin for this recipe. If you are making the custard yourself with custard powder make up approx. half a pint according to the instructions on the tin, but leave out a little of the milk to thicken it slightly.

Spread the jam over the pastry case in a thick layer.

Slice the banana and place on top of jam.

Once the custard has cooled slightly, pour over the jam and bananas.

Sprinkle with desiccated coconut.

Place in fridge to set.

BUTTERSCOTCH TART

Ingredients:

35g plain flour
175g unsalted butter
100ml milk
175g soft brown sugar

1 readymade shortcrust pastry case **OR**

200g plain flour
100g butter or margarine chilled
2 tbsp cold water

To make the pastry:
Place 200g plain flour into a bowl. Chop the butter
into small pieces (or grate) and add it to the bowl.
Rub the butter into the flour until it resembles
breadcrumbs.

Add the cold water gradually, mixing with a round
ended knife until the mixture starts to come
together. Knead lightly making sure all the flour is
incorporated from inside the bowl and then turn out
onto a floured surface.

Roll out the dough until it approximately 5cm larger
than an 18cm sandwich tin. Drape the pastry over
the rolling pin and place over the tin. Press the
pastry down into the corners of the tin but do not
cut off the excess pastry. Place in the fridge to chill
for half an hour.
Heat the oven to 200C/Gas Mark 6/400F.

Place baking beans into the baking case or if you do not have baking beans cut out a square of greaseproof paper, place it over the pastry and weight it down with dried beans or rice.

Bake for 15 minutes, then remove the beans or rice and bake for a further 5 minutes.

To make the filling:
Place the butter and most of the milk in a saucepan. Heat over a low heat until the butter is melted.

Add the sugar and the remaining milk. Stir the mixture well until it comes together.

Sieve 35g plain flour and whisk it in little by little. Ensure you add it gradually and stir it well over a low heat to prevent lumps.

Once the flour is added let the mixture bubble away for a minute or so. Let the mixture cool slightly before pouring into your pastry case. Savour the memories!

CHOCOLATE CRACKOLATE / CORNFLAKE CAKE

Ingredients:

150g Margarine
100g Caster Sugar
110g Golden Syrup
30g Cocoa Powder
175g Cornflakes or Rice Krispies

Method:

Melt the margarine, sugar, syrup and cocoa powder together in a pan over a low heat. Stir well until the sugar is dissolved. Add the cornflakes or rice krispies.

Drop mounds of the mixture into paper cake cases and leave in the fridge to set. Alternatively press the mixture down into a square tin and cut into slices when chilled.

For added 70's authenticity, serve with mint custard!

SPOTTED DICK

Ingredients: Serves 4-6

250g self-raising flour
125g shredded suet
90g caster sugar
125g sultanas
Rind of ½ a lemon finely grated

Method:

You will need a buttered 2-pint pudding basin and a method of steaming the pudding. If you don't have a steamer a wire rack on the base of a saucepan with a tight fitting lid will work well. Avoid the basin sitting directly on the pan base.

Sieve the flour into a bowl and add the suet. Stir in the sultanas, sugar and the lemon rind. Add enough water (about 150ml) to make a soft dropping consistency. Avoid adding too much water or the pudding will be heavy instead of soft and springy.

Spoon the mixture into the pudding basin. Cut some baking parchment or greaseproof paper and add a pleat in the middle to allow for expansion.

This should be just bigger than the edge of the basin.
Cover the bowl with foil and scrunch around the edges to form a seal. Alternatively, secure with a rubber band.

Place the basin into the steamer or prepared pan. Fill the steamer with boiling water to come up to around 2/3 of the sides of the pudding basin. Place the lid on the steamer or basin.

Steam for around 2 hours or until the pudding springs back when pressed. Check the water level regularly to ensure that it does not boil dry.

Serve with custard or for a twist, spoon over Golden Syrup.

SEMOLINA PUDDING

Probably one of the most loathed of all British school meals, "soggy semolina" is included here for posterity.

Ingredients:

568ml (1pint) milk
45g semolina
25g caster sugar
15g butter

To serve, a splodge of jam, freshly grated nutmeg or old school jam sauce – recipe on the next page.

Method:

Preheat the oven to 160C/Gas Mark 3/325F.

Grease an ovenproof dish

Place the milk into a pan and heat until barely warm.

Add the semolina. Stir well. Bring to the boil, stirring well until the mixture thickens.

Add the sugar and butter.

Pour into the ovenproof dish

Sprinkle over nutmeg if using or dollop jam into the middle.

Bake for 30 minutes.

JAM SAUCE

Usually served with semolina, but occasionally the dinner lady would let us eat it on its own!

Ingredients:

1 jar seedless strawberry or raspberry jam.
¼ cup water

Method:

Put the jam and water into a saucepan.

Stir over a low heat until the jam melts.

Add more or less water depending on the consistency required.

TAPIOCA PUDDING

Voted the worst school pudding ever in a poll, Tapioca or "frogspawn" as it was known by generations of school kids, still has one or two die-hard fans.

Ingredients:

50g tapioca *
568ml (1 pint) fresh milk
2 tbsp sugar
15g butter
¼ tsp cinnamon, nutmeg or mixed spice

*Note: Some forms of tapioca require soaking overnight. If this is the case, follow the instructions on the packet and omit a little of the milk in this recipe.

Method:

Place the tapioca in a buttered 2-pint ovenproof serving dish. Pour in the milk

Add sugar and butter. Top with cinnamon, nutmeg or mixed spice.

Bake at 160C/Gas Mark 3/325F for 2 ½ hours stirring twice during the first hour.

BAKEWELL TART

Ingredients:

For the pastry:
225g plain flour
150g butter chilled
25g icing sugar
1 large egg beaten

For the filling:
150g butter softened
150g caster sugar
150g ground almonds
1 large egg beaten
1tsp almond extract
3-4 tbsp raspberry jam

For the icing (optional)
300g icing sugar
1 tsp almond extract

Method:

Make the pastry. Place the flour into a bowl and rub in 150g butter until the mixture resembles breadcrumbs. Stir in 25g icing sugar.

Add the egg and gradually add around 2tbsp water mixing with a round ended knife until the dough comes together.

Turn onto a floured board and roll out to a 3mm thickness. Line a 23mm fluted flan tin and put in the fridge to chill.

Preheat the oven to 200C/Gas Mark 6/400FLine the pasty case with non-stick paper or baking parchment and fill with ceramic baking beans. If you do not have these dried beans or rice will do.

Bake blind for 15 minutes then remove the beans and cook for a further 5 minutes. Remove from the oven and allow to cool slightly. Turn down the oven to 180C/Gas Mark 4/350F

Spread the raspberry jam over the base of the pastry case.

Cream 150g butter and 150g caster sugar together until fluffy. Add 1 egg, the almonds and 1 tsp almond extract. Mix until smooth. Place the mixture into the pastry case and bake for around 30 minutes. Allow to cool completely.

If you are icing your Bakewell Tart, sieve the icing sugar into a bowl. Add the almond extract and enough of the cold water to make a fairly thick icing that coats the back of a spoon. Spread over the cooled tart.

To make the characteristic pattern on top of your tart, pipe lines of icing in a contrasting colour across the tart. Then drag a cocktail stick (at a right angle) through the lines.

JAM ROLY POLY

Ingredients: (Serves 4)

175g self-raising flour
15g butter plus a little extra for greasing
2 tbsp caster sugar
75g shredded suet
115ml milk
125g strawberry or raspberry jam
pinch of salt

Method:

Preheat the oven to 200C/Gas Mark 6/400F. Place a wire rack over a roasting tin. Cut 35cm lengths from a roll of baking paper and a roll of foil. Grease the baking paper and make a pleat in the middle.

Sieve the flour and the salt into a bowl. Rub in the butter. Stir in the suet and the sugar.

Add the milk and mix with a knife to form a soft dough. Roll out on a floured surface to a 25cm by 30cm rectangle.

Spread the jam onto the dough leaving a small gap of 1cm all the way around. Moisten this edge with water.
Roll up the dough from the short side, rather like a Swiss Roll. Press the edges together to form a seal

then place onto the greased baking paper. Roll up loosely leaving room for the roly poly to expand.

Loosely wrap the foil around the roly poly and pinch the edges together.

Fill the roasting tin about one thirds full with boiling water. Place the roly poly onto the wire rack ensuring that it does not touch the water.

Place in the oven and bake for 45 minutes:

Note: To make "dead man's leg" which is an alternate version of roly poly do not wrap the pudding. Instead place directly on a baking tray and brush the top with milk. The pastry will crack and the jam will ooze out giving the appearance of a dead man's leg. Sprinkle with sugar when baked.

JAM AND COCONUT SPONGE

Ingredients:

225g self-raising flour
225g butter, softened, plus extra for greasing
225g caster sugar
4 eggs
1/2 tsp baking powder
25ml milk
1 tsp vanilla extract
75g desiccated coconut
150g strawberry jam

Method:

Preheat oven to 180C/Gas Mark 4/350F. Grease a
30 x 20cm tin.

Cream together the butter and sugar until pale and
fluffy. Add the eggs one by one with a spoonful of
flour with each. Fold in the remaining flour and
baking powder, then stir in the vanilla extract and
milk.

Turn into the prepared tin and bake for 30 minutes
or until a skewer comes out clean.

When the cake is cool, spread over the jam and
sprinkle on desiccated coconut. Cut into squares.

APPLE PIE

Ingredients:

For the pastry:
150g plain flour
75g butter or margarine
1 tbsp caster sugar
2-3 tbsp cold water
milk to glaze
sugar to sprinkle on top.

Filling:
I large cooking apple, washed, peeled and cored.
50g sugar

Method:

Preheat the oven to 200C/Gas Mark 7/425F.

Sieve the flour into a bowl. Cut the butter or margarine into small pieces and rub into the flour until it resembles fine breadcrumbs.

Using a round bladed knife, stir in the sugar and then enough water to make a soft but not sticky dough.

Roll out on a floured surface and then divide the pastry into two. Use one half to line a pie dish or ovenproof plate.

Slice the apple then layer onto the pastry, sprinkling with sugar between layer.

Roll out the remaining pastry to form a lid for the pie. Wet the edges of the pastry and crimp or pinch together to form a seal.

Brush the top of the pie with a little milk. Place in the oven and bake for 20-25 minutes or until golden brown. Remove from the oven and sprinkle with sugar.

TREACLE TART

Ingredients:

175g shortcrust pastry (see note)
3 rounded tbsp Golden Syrup
1 tsp grated lemon rind
2 rounded tbsp fresh white breadcrumbs

Method:

Preheat the oven to 190C/Gas Mark 5/375F

Grease an over-proof plate or shallow pie dish.
Roll out three quarters of the pastry retaining the
rest to make the characteristic lattice pattern on top
of the tart.

Use the rolled out pastry to line the pie dish.   Prick
the bottom of the tart with a fork.

In a saucepan, warm the syrup and lemon rind, stir
in the breadcrumbs and pour the mixture over the
pastry base.

Roll out the remaining pastry and cut into strips of
approximately 1cm wide. Arrange these over the
tart to form a lattice pattern.

Damp the edges of the pastry with a little water and
press the strips down to seal.

Bake in the centre of the oven for approx. 30
minutes or until the pastry is golden brown.

Notes:

<u>To Make 175g Short Crust Pastry:</u>

175g plain flour
100g butter cut into cubes
3 tbsp cold water
pinch of salt.

Place the flour, salt and butter into a bowl.

Rub the butter into the flour using your fingertips until the mixture resembles breadcrumbs.

Mix in enough water with a round bladed knife until the mixture starts to come together.

Gather into a ball and knead gently but be careful not to overwork.

Rest the pastry in the fridge for 30 minutes.

JAM TART

Ingredients:

175g shortcrust pastry (see recipe for treacle tart)
5 tbsp jam

Method:

Preheat the oven to 190C/Gas Mark 5/375F.
Grease an over-proof plate or shallow pie dish.

Roll out the pastry thinly and line your plate or pie
dish. Trim the excess pastry from around the edge.

Spread the jam over the pastry leaving a 1cm gap
around the edge. As the tart cooks the jam will
bubble and expand and this gap will help to stop it
from flowing over the edge of the pastry.

If you wish, use the excess pastry trimmings to
make a pattern on the top of the tart.

Bake in the centre of the oven for approx. 30
minutes or until the pastry is golden brown.

BREAD AND BUTTER PUDDING

Ingredients:

6 slices white bread
50g butter
50g mixed dried fruit
50g caster sugar
3 eggs
1 pint milk

Method:

Remove the crusts from the bread and spread thickly with butter. Cut each slice diagonally into four triangles.

Butter a 2-pint rectangular oven proof dish. Layer the bread over the bottom of the dish, butter side up and sprinkle with some of the fruit and sugar.

Arrange another layer of bread, sprinkle with the remaining fruit and half of the sugar.

Place the remaining bread on top of this and sprinkle on the remaining sugar.

Beat the eggs and add them to the milk. Pour over the pudding.

Leave the pudding to stand for half an hour to allow the liquid to be absorbed.

Heat the oven to 170C/Gas Mark 3/325F.

Bake or 45-60 minutes or until the top is crisp and golden brown.

Variation. For an orangey twist on the traditional pudding spread the buttered bread with marmalade.

COLLEGE PUDDING

Ingredients:

50g self-raising flour
50g brown bread crumbs
50g shredded suet
100g dried fruit
25g brown sugar
1/2 tsp mixed spice
1 egg beaten
60ml milk

Method:

Grease a 1 ½ pint pudding basin and prepare a steamer. A wire rack on the base of a saucepan with a tight fitting lid will suffice if you don't have a steamer.

Mix together the flour, breadcrumbs, suet, dried fruit, sugar and spice. Add the egg and milk.

Turn into the pudding basin, cover the basin tightly with foil and secure with string.

Steam for 2 – 2 ½ hours. Allow the pudding to shrink back slightly before turning out.

NEW COLLEGE PUDDING

This is a shallow or deep fried (depending on your preference) version of the traditional college pudding recipe.

Ingredients:

1 cup dried bread crumbs
1 cup shredded suet
½ - 1 cup mixed dried fruit.
finely grated zest of 1 lemon
½ teaspoon mixed spice
2 eggs

Method:

Mix together the bread crumbs, suet, fruit, lemon zest and spice.

Beat the eggs and add enough egg to the mixture to make a stiff-ish dough, firm enough to be shaped.

Flour your hands and form the mixture into small balls around 3cm across.

Melt a little butter in a frying pan and fry the dough

balls until brown and cooked all the way through.

Alternatively, deep fry the puddings in hot oil.

Traditionally, these puddings were served with a sherry sauce made of equal parts of butter, sugar and sherry.

Alternatively, you can sprinkle with sugar or serve drizzled with Golden Syrup.

QUEEN OF PUDDINGS

Ingredients:

75g fresh white breadcrumbs
25g granulated sugar
rind of one lemon finely grated
25g butter
450ml milk
2 eggs (separated)
2 tbsp raspberry jam
50g caster sugar

To decorate:
A little extra caster sugar
glace cherries (optional)

Method:

Mix together the breadcrumbs and granulated sugar. Place the milk, lemon rind and butter in a saucepan and heat gently until the butter melts.

Pour in the breadcrumb mixture. Leave to absorb the liquid for 30 minutes or so.

Preheat the oven to 160C/Gas Mark 3/325F.

Pour the mixture into a greased 1 ½ pint oven proof dish.

Bake in the oven for 30 minutes until set.

Spread the jam over the pudding. Whisk the eggs whites until stiff. Fold the caster sugar into the egg whites and spread over the top of the jam.

Using a fork, swirl the egg white mixture into small peaks. Sprinkle a little more caster sugar over the top and decorate with glace cherries if liked.

Bake for 30 minutes.

OLD FASHIONED GINGERBREAD PUDDING

Ingredients:

100g butter or margarine
175g black treacle
50g golden syrup
50g soft brown sugar
150ml milk
2 beaten eggs
225g plain flour
2 tsp mixed spice
2 tsp ground ginger
1 tsp bicarbonate of soda

Method:

Grease a 20cm cake tin.

Place the butter or margarine, treacle, syrup and sugar into a saucepan and heat gently until melted.

Add the milk, let the mixture cool slightly and then add the beaten eggs.

Preheat the oven to 150C/Gas Mark 2/300F.

Sieve the flour into a bowl, add the spice, ginger

and bicarbonate of soda.

Stir in the syrup mixture and beat well.

Place in the prepared tin place on the middle shelf of the oven. If you are using a fan oven it may be necessary to slightly turn down the temperature.

Bake for 1 ½ hours or until a knife inserted into the centre comes out clean.

JAM SPONGE PUDDING

This is an easy microwaveable version of the traditional steamed jam sponge school pudding. If you want to be truly authentic, go ahead and steam the pudding for 2 hours!

Ingredients:

50g butter
50g caster sugar
50g self-raising flour
1 medium egg, beaten
2 tbsp milk
2 tbsp of jam

Method:

Cream together the butter and sugar until light and fluffy.

Gradually stir in the egg and milk taking care not to curdle the mixture. Fold in the flour.

Spread the jam over the base of a microwave safe basin. Spoon over the sponge mixture.

Cover and microwave on full power for 3 – 4

minutes or until a skewer comes out clean.

Variations:

Golden Syrup – Replace the jam with 2 tbsp
Golden Syrup

Marmalade – Replace the jam with tbsp
marmalade.

Spotted Dick – Stir 50g dried fruit into the mixture.

Lemon – Replace the jam with tbsp lemon curd and
stir the grated rind of a lemon into the mixture.

Chocolate – Use Nutella instead of jam and replace
25g of the flour with cocoa powder.

PINK CUSTARD

Ingredients:

1 pint milk
1 packet pink blancmange mix
2 tbsp sugar

Method:

Empty the blancmange mix into a bowl. Stir in the sugar.

Add a splash or two of the milk to form a paste. Put the remaining milk into a saucepan and heat but don't allow to boil.

Add the blancmange paste to the saucepan with the heated milk and stir well. Keep stirring and bring to the boil.

Once the mixture has thickened, remove from the heat and serve!

CORNFLAKE TART

Ingredients:

<u>For the pastry</u>
180g flour
80g butter or margarine
30ml water

<u>For the filling</u>
110g golden syrup
80g cornflakes
40g margarine
30g sugar
110g strawberry jam

Method:

Preheat the oven to 200C/Gas Mark 6/400F.

To make the pastry, rub the butter or margarine into the flour until it resembles breadcrumbs. Add the water gradually until the pastry comes together. Knead gently.

Roll out the pastry and line a flan dish or sandwich tin. Bake blind for 20 minutes.

In a heavy bottomed saucepan, combine the butter, golden syrup and sugar. Heat gently until melted. Add in the cornflakes and stir well.

Spread the jam over the pastry base and then top with the cornflake mixture.

Return to the oven for 5 minutes to set.

BREAD PUDDING

Ingredients:

one white loaf, turned into breadcrumbs
150 g sugar
500g mixed dried fruit
1 litre milk
75g butter plus a little extra for greasing and dotting on top
2 tsp mixed spice
1 tsp vanilla extract
a little demerara sugar to sprinkle on top

Method:

Preheat the oven to 180C/Gas Mark 4/350F.

Place the butter, milk, sugar and dried fruit into a saucepan. Heat gently until the butter has melted and the sugar has dissolved.

Add the breadcrumbs, mixed spice and vanilla extract and stir well. Turn the mixture into a greased tin, dot a little butter over the top and cover with foil.

Bake for about one hour, removing the foil for the last ten minutes of cooking time.

RAINBOW SPONGE

Ingredients:

200g butter or margarine softened
200g caster sugar
200g self-raising flour
3 eggs
5 tbsp milk

red green and blue food colourings

Method:

Preheat oven to 180C/Gas Mark 4/350F

Cream together the butter and sugar until light and fluffy. Beat in the eggs one by one.

Fold in the flour and enough milk to form a soft consistency which will drop off a spoon.

Divide the mixture into four bowls. Leave one bowl plain and add a few drops of food colouring to the other three so you have red, blue, green and plain (yellow) mixtures.

Dollop spoonful's of the mixture over the bottom of the tin to form a rainbow pattern. Cover the whole tin.

Bake for 35-40 minutes or until the sponge springs back when pressed.

Serve with pink custard for an authentic school treat!

EVES PUDDING

Ingredients:

450g cooking apples, peeled cored and sliced
75g demerara sugar
Finely grated rind of 1 lemon
100g caster sugar
100g butter or margarine
2 eggs beaten
100g self-raising flour
a few drops vanilla essence
sugar for sprinkling

Method:

Preheat the oven to 180C/Gas Mark 4/350F.
Butter an oven proof dish and layer the apples,
sprinkling each layer with lemon rind and demerara
sugar.

Cream the butter and caster sugar together until
fluffy, add the eggs and a few drops of vanilla
essence and fold in the flour.

Spread this mixture over the fruit. Bake for 35-40
minutes until golden brown. Sprinkle a little sugar
over the top before serving.

CHOCOLATE PUDDING WITH CHOCOLATE SAUCE

Ingredients:

For the pudding
75g butter
75g caster sugar
25g cocoa powder
150g self-raising flour
2 eggs
4 tbsp milk

For the chocolate sauce:
20g sugar
20g cornflour
40g dried milk powder
15g cocoa powder
600ml water

Method:

Heat the oven to 180C/Gas Mark 4/350F. Grease a 1 litre oven proof dish.

Cream the butter and 75g caster sugar together until light and fluffy.

Add the eggs one at a time, fold in the flour and cocoa powder and enough milk to form a soft dropping consistency. Spoon into the dish and bake for 35/40 minutes.

Meanwhile make the chocolate sauce.

Place the water and milk powder into a saucepan and mix together.

In a bowl, combine the cocoa, cornflour and sugar and then take a couple of spoonful's of the milk and water mixture to blend the dry ingredients into a thin paste.

Bring the remaining contents of the saucepan to near boiling point and then stir in the cocoa mixture. Bring to the boil stirring all the time.

Cook for a couple of minutes then remove from the heat and pour into a jug. Cover until ready to use. Serve with the warm sponge.

RHUBARB CRUMBLE

Ingredients:

500g rhubarb, trimmed and sliced into 3cm pieces
100g caster sugar
200g plain flour
100g cold butter, cubed
125g demerara sugar

Method:

Preheat the oven to 180C/Gas Mark 4/350F. Put the rhubarb into a 1.2 l oven proof dish and sprinkle over the caster sugar. Pour in 50ml cold water.

Place the flour into a bowl and rub in the butter until the mixture resembles breadcrumbs. Stir in the demerara sugar.

Spread the crumble mixture over the rhubarb. Bake for 45 minutes until the crumble is brown and the rhubarb is soft.

COUNTRY MINCEMEAT TART

Ingredients:

175g self-raising flour
40g caster sugar
50g butter
1 egg beaten
5 tbsp mincemeat or jam

Method:

Preheat the oven to 200C/Gas Mark 6/400F

Rub the butter into the flour until it resembles breadcrumbs. Stir in the sugar. Add the egg and a little water to form a firm dough. Divide into two.

On a floured board roll each piece into a rectangle the size of your baking sheet. Spread with mincemeat leaving a gap around the edges to seal.

Moisten the edges and place the second rectangle on top. Pinch the edges together well to seal.

Bake for 20 minutes until golden brown, sprinkle with caster sugar and serve, cut into squares with custard.

GYPSY TART

Ingredients:

225g shortcrust pastry or a ready-made pastry shell
400g tin evaporated milk
350g dark muscovado sugar.

Method:

Preheat the oven to 200C/Gas Mark 6/400F

Line a 27cm flan dish with the pastry. Cut out a circle of greaseproof paper, lay over the pastry and fill with ceramic baking beans or dried beans or lentils.

Bake blind for 15-20 minutes and then allow the pastry to cool.

Whip the evaporated milk and sugar together for 10 minutes or until well blended. Pour this into the cooled pastry case and pop in the oven for 10 minute until set.

Remove from the oven and allow to cool. Serve with blobs of "mock cream".

MOCK CREAM/DREAM TOPPING

Remember those little blobs of mock cream which were piped on top of your dessert?

Ingredients:

50g margarine
50g caster sugar
2 tbsp hot water
2 tbsp hot milk

Method:

Cream together the margarine and sugar until light and fluffy.

 Beat the milk in drop by drop and add enough water to give the consistency you desire.

Allow to cool and place in a piping bag.

SQUASHED FLY PIE

Ingredients:

175g shortcrust pastry
150g seedless raisins
¼ tsp bicarbonate of soda
4 tbsp hot water
50g soft brown sugar

For the topping:
100g plain flour
½ tsp ground cinnamon
¼ tsp ground ginger
¼ tsp ground nutmeg
50g butter
50g soft brown sugar

Method:

Preheat the oven to 220C/Gas Mark 7/425F.

Roll out the pastry to line a 20cm flan dish or pie plate. Prick the pastry base and cover with raisins.

Mix together the water, sugar and bicarbonate of soda. Pour this mixture over the raisins.

Sift the flour into a bowl together with the ginger, cinnamon and nutmeg. Rub in the butter until the mixture resembles fine breadcrumbs and then stir in the sugar.

Spread the flour mixture over the top of the raisins then bake in the oven for 10 minutes until the pie begins to brown.

Reduce the oven temperature to 160C/Gas Mark 3/325F. Bake for another 20 minutes or until the filling is set.

Serve warm with custard.

Quick Metric To Imperial Conversion:

10g – ½ oz
25g – 1oz
50g – 2oz
110g – 4oz
175g – 6oz
225g – 8oz
450g – 1 lb
900g – 2lb

Printed in Great Britain
by Amazon

55289110R00046